THE AIDS CRISIS

BY KATIE KAWA

Gareth Stevens
PUBLISHING

Please visit our website, www.garethstevens.com. For a free color catalog of all our high-quality books, call toll free 1-800-542-2595 or fax 1-877-542-2596.

Library of Congress Cataloging-in-Publication Data

Names: Kawa, Katie, author.
Title: The AIDS crisis / Katie Kawa.
Description: New York : Gareth Stevens Publishing, [2019] | Series: History just before you were born | Includes index.
Identifiers: LCCN 2018022954| ISBN 9781538230251 (library bound) | ISBN 9781538231623 (pbk.) | ISBN 9781538233207 (6 pack)
Subjects: LCSH: AIDS (Disease)--History--Juvenile literature.
Classification: LCC RA644.A25 K39 2019 | DDC 362.19697/92--dc23
LC record available at https://lccn.loc.gov/2018022954

First Edition

Published in 2019 by
Gareth Stevens Publishing
111 East 14th Street, Suite 349
New York, NY 10003

Copyright © 2019 Gareth Stevens Publishing

Designer: Sarah Liddell
Editor: Therese Shea

Photo credits: Cover, p. 1 Allan Tannenbaum/Contributor/Archive Photos/Getty Images; newspaper text background used throughout EddieCloud/Shutterstock.com; newspaper shape used throughout AVS-Images/Shutterstock.com; newspaper texture used throughout Here/Shutterstock.com; halftone texture used throughout xpixel/Shutterstock.com; pp. 5, 11, 13, 15 (main and inset) Bettmann/Contributor/Bettmann/Getty Images; p. 7 David Paul Morris/Stringer/Getty Images News/Getty Images; p. 9 (main) GERARD CERLES/Staff/AFP/Getty Images; p. 9 (inset) BSIP/Contributor/Universal Images Group/Getty Images; p. 17 Peter Gridley/The Image Bank/Getty Images; p. 19 Tim Graham/Contributor/Tim Graham Photo Library/Getty Images; p. 21 SGranitz/Contributor/WireImage/Getty Images; p. 23 Joe Raedle/Staff/Getty Images News/Getty Images; p. 25 MATTHEW KAY/Stringer/AFP80/Getty Images; p. 27 (main and inset) ALEXANDER JOE/Staff/AFP/Getty Images; p. 28 Jeff Greenberg/Contributor/Universal Images Group/Getty Images.

Printed in the United States of America

CONTENTS

Words in the glossary appear in **bold** type
the first time they are used in the text.

A DEADLY DISEASE

Mysterious sicknesses with no cure are the subject of some scary movies. However, they're also a part of the real world. In the 1980s, thousands of people began dying because of a disease scientists knew very little about. Today, this disease is known as acquired immunodeficiency syndrome or, more commonly, AIDS.

The spread of AIDS was a health **crisis** that changed the world. People became very afraid of the disease—and of those who might have it. As time went on and scientists discovered more about AIDS, some of that fear went away. In fact, many began to believe the AIDS crisis was over. However, millions of people around the world are still affected by this deadly disease, and scientists are still searching for a cure.

MORE TO THE STORY

An epidemic is the quick spread of a disease that affects many people at the same time. The AIDS epidemic has led to the death of more than 35 million people around the world.

IT'S IMPORTANT TO LEARN HOW THE AIDS CRISIS BEGAN BECAUSE THIS DISEASE STILL AFFECTS MILLIONS OF PEOPLE AROUND THE WORLD.

WHY IS AIDS DEADLY?

AIDS affects the immune system, which is the part of the body that fights diseases. It damages a person's immune system until their body can't protect itself anymore. It becomes easier for the person to fall ill. People with AIDS often die of diseases that their bodies can't fight on their own. These include certain kinds of **cancer** and other sicknesses known as opportunistic **infections**, which are only a danger to people with weak immune systems.

5

THE CRISIS BEGINS

The first official report about what became known as AIDS was published on June 5, 1981. This report, from the US Centers for Disease Control and Prevention (CDC), described a rare lung infection and other signs of weakened immune systems present in a group of five men in Los Angeles, California. Although the doctors didn't know it yet, they were describing a group of people who had AIDS.

The next year, this mysterious sickness was given a name. On September 24, 1982, the CDC used the term "AIDS" for the first time to describe the immune system condition. Earlier that same year, the first clinic to help people with AIDS was set up in San Francisco, California.

MORE TO THE STORY

The first people reported to have AIDS were adult men. However, in December 1982, reports came out about babies with AIDS, and in 1983, it was discovered that women could also have AIDS.

Most scientists believe AIDS came from Africa. It most likely started in chimpanzees in the early 1900s. People often hunted these animals at that time. Some scientists believe the virus that causes AIDS spread from chimpanzees to humans when infected chimpanzee blood got into an open cut on a human hunter. Others believe it happened when a person ate the meat of an infected chimpanzee. This may have happened in the 1920s in what is now the Democratic Republic of Congo.

SAN FRANCISCO, CALIFORNIA, WAS HIT HARD BY THE AIDS CRISIS. VISITORS TO THE CITY'S NATIONAL AIDS MEMORIAL GROVE CAN SEE THE CIRCLE OF FRIENDS, WHICH IS FILLED WITH NAMES OF PEOPLE WHO DIED FROM AIDS-RELATED ILLNESSES AND OTHERS WHO HAVE BEEN AFFECTED BY THE DISEASE.

DISCOVERING THE CAUSE

As the number of people with AIDS began to rise, doctors continued to search for the cause of this disease. Finding the cause would make it easier to discover how AIDS was spreading and how it could be treated.

In 1983, French scientists, including Luc Montagnier and Françoise Barré-Sinoussi, discovered a kind of virus known as a retrovirus that they called LAV. They believed this virus caused AIDS, and they worked to study this connection, with the help of US scientists such as Robert Gallo.

By 1985, the CDC had reported that this virus caused AIDS, and blood tests for the virus began in the United States that year. However, it wasn't until the next year that the virus was officially given a name: the human immunodeficiency virus, which is more commonly known as HIV.

MORE TO THE STORY

In 2008, Françoise Barré-Sinoussi and Luc Montagnier won a Nobel Prize for the part they played in discovering HIV. Barré-Sinoussi said, "I hope that this recognition will provide the necessary spark to spur international efforts in the fight against HIV/AIDS."

LUC MONTAGNIER (LEFT) AND FRANÇOISE BARRÉ-SINOUSSI (RIGHT) PLAYED A BIG PART IN THE DISCOVERY OF HIV AND CONTINUE TO DO IMPORTANT WORK TO FIGHT AIDS AROUND THE WORLD.

HIV VIRUS

THE SPREAD OF HIV

In the early years of the AIDS crisis, scientists discovered how the disease spread. HIV, which causes AIDS, can only be spread directly through bodily fluids, such as blood. If a pregnant woman has HIV, she can pass it on to her baby. It spreads through sexual contact as well. This is why the development of a blood test for HIV was so important. Once people know they have the virus, they can keep themselves from spreading it to others.

HELPING EACH OTHER

At the beginning of the AIDS crisis, one group was affected in greater numbers than any other: gay men. In fact, before AIDS was known by that name, it was sometimes called GRID, which stood for "gay-related immune deficiency." Some people even called it the "gay plague" and believed it was a kind of punishment for gay men, who faced many kinds of **discrimination** at that time.

The connection between AIDS and the gay community created a **stigma** around the disease. Some people—even some doctors—didn't want to help or care for those with AIDS because they didn't like gay people. Members of the gay community came together and took care of each other during this time.

> **MORE TO THE STORY**
>
> By the end of 1983, men who'd been in relationships with other men made up 71 percent of all reported AIDS cases.

DURING THE EARLY YEARS OF THE AIDS CRISIS, MANY GAY MEN LOST THEIR LIVES BECAUSE OF THIS DISEASE, AND MANY LOST FRIENDS AND PARTNERS. THOUGH OFTEN TREATED UNFAIRLY AND UNKINDLY, THEY STAYED STRONG AND HELPED EACH OTHER.

AIDS AND DRUGS

AIDS also affects drug users. Because HIV is spread through direct contact with blood, sharing needles with another person is one way to catch the virus. Some people who use certain kinds of illegal drugs share needles to put the drugs into their body. If one of these people has HIV, they can spread the virus to others who use their needles. Because people who use illegal drugs are doing something against the law, some saw AIDS as a punishment for them, too.

RYAN WHITE'S BRAVE BATTLE

Although many people continued to believe AIDS was a disease that only affected gay men, stories began spreading about other people getting sick. One of the most famous involved a brave young man who fought to have a normal life.

Ryan White was 13 years old in 1984 when he was **diagnosed** with AIDS. He still wanted to go to school, but people in his town were afraid of him and treated him poorly. After his family moved to a new town, he was able to attend school and even get a job. Ryan helped make the world a better place before he died in 1990. He opened many people's eyes to the fact that people with AIDS are just like everyone else and deserve to be treated with compassion.

MORE TO THE STORY

In August 1990, US Congress passed an act that provided more than $220 million for HIV and AIDS treatment. It was named the Ryan White Comprehensive AIDS Resources Emergency (CARE) Act.

RYAN WHITE ONCE SAID, "I CAME FACE TO FACE WITH DEATH AT 13 YEARS OLD." AT FIRST, HE WAS ONLY GIVEN A FEW MONTHS TO LIVE, BUT HE LIVED TO BE 18. HIS FIGHT TO BE TREATED FAIRLY WAS A MAJOR TURNING POINT IN HOW PEOPLE VIEWED AIDS AND THOSE WHO LIVED WITH IT.

BLOOD TRANSFUSIONS AND AIDS

Ryan White's mother said people believed "he had done something he shouldn't have done or he wouldn't have gotten AIDS." Ryan had hemophilia, a disease that causes a person who has been cut or injured to bleed for a long time. Ryan got AIDS after he was exposed to HIV through a blood transfusion, which is the transferring of blood from one person to another. In 1985, donated blood began to be tested for HIV.

SILENCE IN WASHINGTON

Ryan White and other people with AIDS spoke with government leaders to educate them about the crisis. Many people with AIDS believed the US government, led by President Ronald Reagan, wasn't doing enough to help them, and even some in the government agreed.

In 1983, a congressional report stated the government was failing to provide proper funding to study and treat AIDS. One of the most outspoken members of Congress on this issue was Henry Waxman, who represented Los Angeles. In 1985, Waxman said, "It is surprising that the president could remain silent as 6,000 Americans died, that he could fail to acknowledge the epidemic's existence." As the crisis got worse, more people began to criticize the government for doing too little.

MORE TO THE STORY

By the time President Reagan shared his 1987 address about AIDS, more than 20,000 Americans had died because of the disease.

LIVING with AIDS
2 yrs 6 mos + counting!
NO THANKS TO YOU
MR REAGAN

DURING THE 1980s, MANY GROUPS
PROTESTED THE US GOVERNMENT'S
SLOW RESPONSE TO THE AIDS CRISIS.

AMERICAN
FOUNDATION
FOR AIDS
RESEARCH

RONALD REAGAN

REAGAN ADDRESSES AIDS

President Ronald Reagan addressed the AIDS crisis in a speech in 1987.
In that speech, he called the disease "public health enemy No. 1," which
meant he saw it as the most important public health problem in the United
States. However, he also suggested the issue was a moral one and could be
combatted with morality. Some criticized Reagan for this view and wished
he had spoken out against **homophobic** reactions to the epidemic.

MAKING A MEMORIAL

As the AIDS crisis continued to claim more lives, people began to look for ways to honor those who died. They wanted to be sure their loved ones who lost their battle with this deadly disease would be remembered. Many also wanted to make a public statement about all the lives that had been lost while the US government failed to act.

The NAMES Project AIDS Memorial Quilt started as a way to accomplish these goals. Most panels, or squares, of this quilt were created to represent someone who lost their battle with AIDS. In 1987, the quilt was displayed on the **National Mall** in Washington, DC, with 1,920 panels. Since that day, the quilt has continued to grow. As of 2018, the quilt consists of more than 48,000 panels.

MORE TO THE STORY

Beginning in 1991, people who have wanted to show support for those living with AIDS sometimes wear a red ribbon on their clothing.

PARTS OF THE NAMES PROJECT AIDS MEMORIAL QUILT
TRAVEL AROUND THE WORLD TO RAISE AIDS AWARENESS.
THE ENTIRE QUILT HAS ONLY BEEN DISPLAYED ON THE
NATIONAL MALL IN WASHINGTON, DC.

WORLD AIDS DAY

In 1988, the World Health Organization (WHO)—a group that works to improve people's health around the world—established the first World AIDS Day. This day is meant to increase awareness about the disease and to encourage countries to share what they know about it with each other. World AIDS Day has been held on December 1 every year, and many groups and businesses raise money for HIV and AIDS research on this day.

FEARS OVER FACTS

Throughout the 1980s, the number of people with AIDS kept rising, and people's fears about the disease kept rising, too. By 1989, it was reported that 100,000 people in the United States had AIDS. For a long time, people held false beliefs about AIDS, which caused them to treat people with the disease poorly.

Many people weren't educated about what caused AIDS or how it spread, so they believed it spread like some other sicknesses. They thought they could get AIDS if someone with the disease coughed on them or even if they shook hands with someone who had it. This made them afraid of people suffering from AIDS. As education has improved over time, people have learned that you can't catch AIDS the way you catch a cold or the flu.

MORE TO THE STORY

In 1987, people with HIV were banned from traveling or moving to the United States. However, President Barack Obama officially lifted this ban in 2010.

A PRINCESS'S KINDNESS

In April 1987, Princess Diana of Wales helped open the first official AIDS unit at a hospital in the United Kingdom. While she was there, she shook the hand of a man who had AIDS without wearing gloves. This was an important moment because it helped prove to people that it wasn't dangerous to touch someone with the disease. Diana said, "You can shake their hands and give them a hug. Heaven knows they need it."

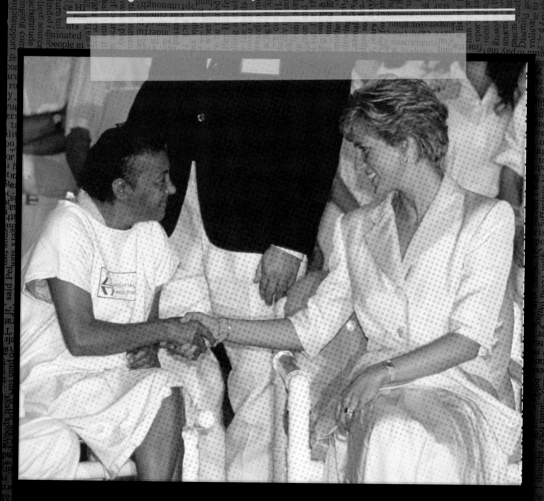

BECAUSE PEOPLE OFTEN DIDN'T KNOW THE FACTS ABOUT HIV AND AIDS, THEY BELIEVED INFECTED PEOPLE WERE DANGEROUS. PRINCESS DIANA (RIGHT) USED HER FAME TO EDUCATE OTHERS ABOUT THE INCORRECT BELIEF THAT HIV AND AIDS COULD EASILY SPREAD TO OTHERS.

MAGIC MAKES A DIFFERENCE

Ryan White and other famous AIDS **activists** in the 1980s did their part to raise awareness about the disease. Then, on November 7, 1991, superstar basketball player Earvin "Magic" Johnson announced he had tested positive for HIV. That announcement opened the door to a new era in AIDS activism.

Magic Johnson was one of the most famous athletes in the world, and he didn't let the fact that he had HIV slow him down. In fact, he played on the US men's basketball team—often called "the Dream Team"—at the 1992 Olympics. Johnson showed the world that a positive HIV test wasn't a death sentence. More than 20 years after his announcement, he continues to be an outspoken activist in the fight against HIV and AIDS.

MORE TO THE STORY

Magic Johnson served on the National Commission on AIDS, which was set up to create a plan to fight the disease. However, he stepped down in 1992. He said President George H. W. Bush and his staff weren't doing enough. The government had "dropped the ball."

MAGIC JOHNSON CONTINUES TO RAISE MONEY AND AWARENESS FOR PEOPLE LIVING WITH HIV AND AIDS. HE HAS SPOKEN OPENLY AND HONESTLY ABOUT THE IMPORTANCE OF BEING TESTED FOR HIV.

LIVING WITH HIV

When Magic Johnson first announced he'd tested positive for HIV, he said, "I just want to make clear, first of all, I do not have the AIDS disease." Thanks to Johnson, people began to understand that being HIV positive and having AIDS aren't the same thing. AIDS is the last stage of HIV infection. People can live for many years with HIV without ever getting AIDS, and they're able to live fairly normal lives.

LIFESAVING TREATMENTS

Magic Johnson discovered he was HIV-positive at a time when things were beginning to change in the fight against HIV and AIDS. In 1987, the US Food and Drug Administration (FDA) approved the first drug to treat HIV. This drug, known as AZT, is part of a group of antiretroviral drugs, which work to keep HIV retrovirus levels low.

AZT alone didn't always work well because HIV can quickly become resistant to it. In 1995, a new kind of treatment, which combined different antiretroviral drugs, was introduced. It's known as highly active antiretroviral therapy (HAART). HAART is considered to be one of the biggest breakthroughs in the fight against AIDS. It's allowed people with HIV to live longer, healthier lives.

> ## MORE TO THE STORY
>
> HAART can lower the levels of HIV in a person's body to the point that they're undetectable, or unable to be measured by tests. This means HAART is working. It doesn't mean a person is cured, but it does lower the chance of a person spreading HIV to someone else.

ANTIRETROVIRAL DRUGS

A retrovirus is a virus with RNA genetic material. The virus uses certain **enzymes** to turn RNA into viral DNA, which then becomes part of the DNA found in human cells. As human DNA is copied to make new proteins, the virus is replicated, or copied, too. The HIV retrovirus attacks immune cells, which is why it weakens the immune system. Antiretroviral drugs work by stopping the enzymes that help the HIV retrovirus make viral DNA.

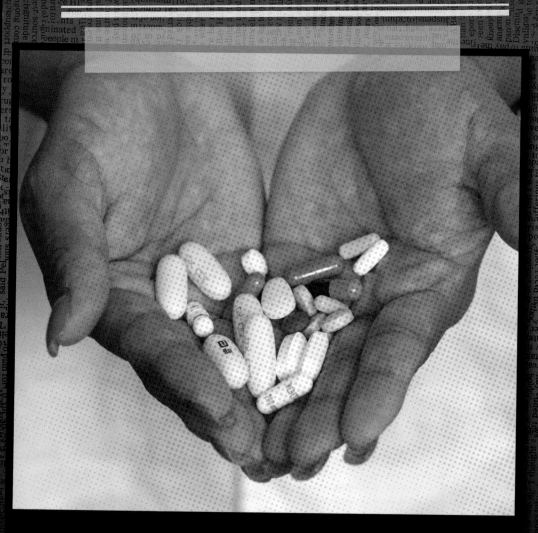

HAART IS SOMETIMES CALLED A "DRUG COCKTAIL" OR THE "AIDS COCKTAIL" BECAUSE IT INVOLVES A MIXTURE OF MANY DIFFERENT DRUGS.

AIDS AROUND THE WORLD

In 1983, the World Health Organization began tracking the spread of AIDS around the planet, and in 1987, it created the Global Program on AIDS. This was an international effort to increase knowledge about the disease, encourage international research, and provide support to individuals suffering from it.

The AIDS crisis has hit poorer countries around the world especially hard. East and southern Africa are the most affected regions. As of 2016, more than 19 million people in this part of the world were living with HIV. More than 40 percent of new HIV infections occur there. However, many people are working hard to educate others about the spread of HIV in Africa and save the lives of those living with the virus.

MORE TO THE STORY

About 2.1 million children around the world were living with HIV in 2016. These children are most often infected by mothers who have the virus.

PEOPLE AROUND THE WORLD, INCLUDING PRINCE HARRY
OF WALES (TOP ROW, THIRD FROM RIGHT), HAVE COME
TOGETHER TO FIGHT THE GLOBAL AIDS CRISIS. IN 2016,
AIDS-RELATED ILLNESSES LED TO 1 MILLION DEATHS,
BUT THAT NUMBER HAS BEEN DECREASING.

UNAIDS

The leader in the worldwide fight against HIV and AIDS is an organization
known as UNAIDS. It was created in 1996 as part of the United Nations (UN),
an international group that works to assist people around the world. UNAIDS
brings people from different countries together to plan the best way to stop
the AIDS crisis and help those living with HIV. Its goal is to end the AIDS
"public health threat" by 2030.

A CONTINUING CRISIS

Throughout the early 2000s, progress was made toward ending the AIDS crisis. The number of people taking antiretroviral drugs rose from less than 1 million in 2000 to more than 20 million in 2017. These drugs have helped people with HIV stay healthy instead of getting sick with AIDS. Better protection against the spread of HIV has also helped slow the epidemic.

These positive signs don't mean the crisis is over, though. As of 2018, there's still no cure for HIV and AIDS. Many people, including large numbers of women and children, are still dying because of this disease. These people often don't have **access** to lifesaving antiretroviral drugs. Although there have been many breakthroughs and lives saved since the 1980s, the crisis has continued.

MORE TO THE STORY

In the United States, women make up 20 percent of the total number of people who've gotten sick with AIDS since the crisis began. Around the world, women make up around 52 percent of people with HIV.

AIDS HAS LED TO THE DEATHS OF MILLIONS OF PEOPLE. IT HAS LEFT MANY CHILDREN ORPHANED, OR WITHOUT PARENTS, ESPECIALLY IN AFRICA.

BILL AND MELINDA GATES

BILL AND MELINDA GATES

Two people who are working hard to end the AIDS crisis are **philanthropists** Bill and Melinda Gates. In 2015, they donated almost $6 million to scientists working on a **vaccine** to fight against HIV in the body. Two years later, Bill Gates called for people to join the fight against AIDS: "We need more AIDS heroes—from health care workers and **advocates** to global leaders. Together, we can bring an end to this public health threat."

27

HISTORY IS STILL HAPPENING

The AIDS crisis changed the world in many ways, and it continues to affect people in different countries today. Millions lost their lives as victims of this epidemic, and people are still dying because of AIDS.

The story of the AIDS crisis is also a story of activism. The gay community in the United States joined together to take care of each other as many of their own were dying. This started a new era in the fight for equal treatment for all Americans.

Although the AIDS crisis isn't over yet, there's hope that it could end in the next few decades. This chapter in history is still unfolding, and we all can play a part in how it ends.

MORE TO THE STORY

The first AIDS Walk, which raised money for the fight against HIV and AIDS, was held in 1985. AIDS walks are still organized in many major cities, and people of all ages can take part in them.

HELPING CHILDREN WITH AIDS

Elizabeth Glaser was infected with HIV from a blood transfusion after giving birth. She then passed the virus on to her children before learning she was HIV-positive. In 1988, Elizabeth and two friends started what's become known as the Elizabeth Glaser Pediatric AIDS Foundation. Although Elizabeth and her daughter died from AIDS-related causes, Elizabeth's son is still alive. The foundation continues to work toward a world where no child gets sick with HIV or AIDS.

A TIMELINE OF THE AIDS CRISIS

- **1981:** THE FIRST OFFICIAL REPORT IS PUBLISHED ABOUT MEN SICK WITH WHAT WOULD BECOME KNOWN AS AIDS.
- **1982:** THE CENTERS FOR DISEASE CONTROL AND PREVENTION USES THE TERM "AIDS" FOR THE FIRST TIME.
- **1983:** FRENCH SCIENTISTS DISCOVER THE VIRUS THAT CAUSES AIDS.
- **1985:** BLOOD TESTS BEGIN FOR THE VIRUS THAT CAUSES AIDS.
- **1986:** THE VIRUS THAT CAUSES AIDS IS GIVEN THE OFFICIAL NAME HIV.
- **1987:** AZT IS APPROVED TO TREAT HIV.
- **1988:** THE FIRST WORLD AIDS DAY TAKES PLACE.
- **1990:** RYAN WHITE DIES OF AN AIDS-RELATED CAUSE, AND THE RYAN WHITE CARE ACT IS PASSED.
- **1991:** MAGIC JOHNSON ANNOUNCES THAT HE'S HIV-POSITIVE.
- **1995:** HAART BECOMES A MAJOR PART OF HIV TREATMENT.
- **1996:** UNAIDS IS SET UP TO FIGHT AIDS AROUND THE WORLD.
- **2010:** THE US TRAVEL BAN FOR PEOPLE WITH HIV AND AIDS IS LIFTED.
- **2015:** BILL AND MELINDA GATES DONATE ALMOST $6 MILLION TO HIV VACCINE RESEARCH.
- **2017:** THE NUMBER OF HIV-POSITIVE PEOPLE TAKING ANTIRETROVIRAL DRUGS RISES TO MORE THAN 20 MILLION.

GLOSSARY

access: a way of getting at or to something

activist: one who acts strongly in support of or against an issue or cause

advocate: one who supports or speaks in favor of something or someone

cancer: a disease caused by the uncontrolled growth of cells in the body

crisis: a difficult or dangerous situation that needs serious attention

diagnose: to recognize a disease or illness by examining someone

discrimination: unfairly treating people unequally because of their race or beliefs

enzyme: matter made in the body that helps certain actions necessary for life to occur

homophobic: unreasonable fear of, dislike of, or discrimination against homosexuality

infection: the spread of germs inside the body, causing illness

National Mall: a large park in Washington, DC, that is located near the US Capitol

philanthropist: a wealthy person who gives money and time to make life better for others

stigma: a negative and unfair viewpoint about something

vaccine: a shot that keeps a person from getting a certain sickness

FOR MORE INFORMATION

BOOKS

Furgang, Kathy. *HIV/AIDS*. New York, NY: Rosen Publishing, 2016.

McPartland, Randall. *HIV and AIDS*. New York, NY: Cavendish Square, 2016.

Simons, Rae. *A Kid's Guide to AIDS and HIV*. Vestal, NY: Village Earth Press, 2016.

WEBSITES

A Timeline of HIV and AIDS
www.hiv.gov/hiv-basics/overview/history/hiv-and-aids-timeline
This timeline allows readers to explore important events in the AIDS crisis from the 1980s to the present.

HIV and AIDS
kidshealth.org/en/kids/hiv.html
This website includes facts about HIV and AIDS, including signs of the disease.

The Names Project—AIDS Memorial Quilt
www.aidsquilt.org/
The website of the AIDS Memorial Quilt provides information on how to make a panel and where to see displays.

INDEX